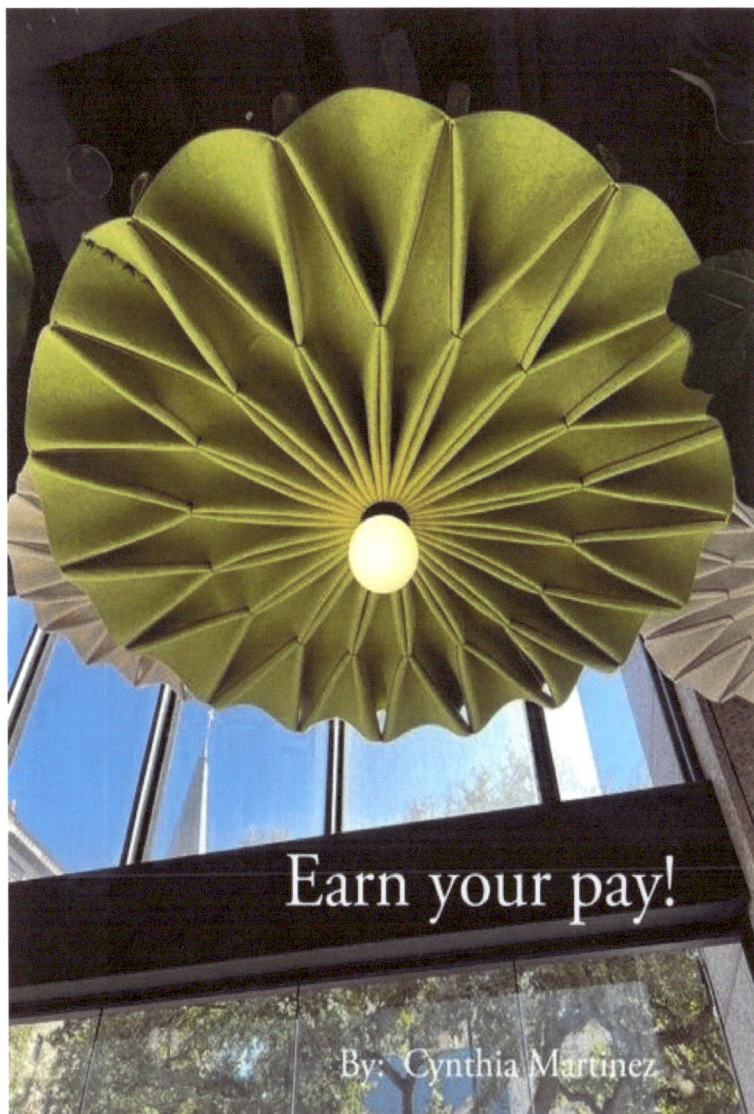

# Earn your pay!

By: Cynthia Martinez

Be the light, when times get dark.

Dedicated to Eric, Monica, Alexis, and Brooke.


Give 100% in everything that you do, and you will be amazed at what you can accomplish!

Be on time!

# Be on Time!

It is your responsibility to be on time. You should show up 15 minutes early to work to ensure being punctual. You know what your work schedule is, make sure that you are prepared. You were hired to work a certain schedule and to report at a certain time. Do not be late!

Dress appropriately!

# Dress Appropriately!

Make sure you are dressed appropriately for work. If you are required to wear a uniform, make sure it is washed and ironed. Wear appropriate shoes, clothing, and be properly groomed. YOUR GOAL IS TO LOOK PROFESSIONAL.

Be ready to work!

# Be ready to work!

Be ready to work! Know your job description. If you are not sure or do not understand your complete job description, make sure you ask on the first day. Do not think that it is ok to stand around doing nothing during work hours. Know what the goals are for the day and give it 100%.

Check your attitude!

Check your attitude!

Having a professional and positive attitude at work is important. It is your job to help create a positive work environment. Meet and greet your customers and co-workers with a smile.

Communication is essential!

# Communication is essential!

Ask, ask, ask, if you don't know, ask! So many people fail at work because they are too afraid to ask a question. It is better to do your job correctly the first time, don't waste your time and energy on a bad job. Make sure the job description has been communicated properly to you. If you are a manager, make sure the employee understands their job description correctly.

Yelling and sarcasm are not proper communication skills. Address a problem immediately, don't wait for it to escalate. Always communicate in a professional manner.

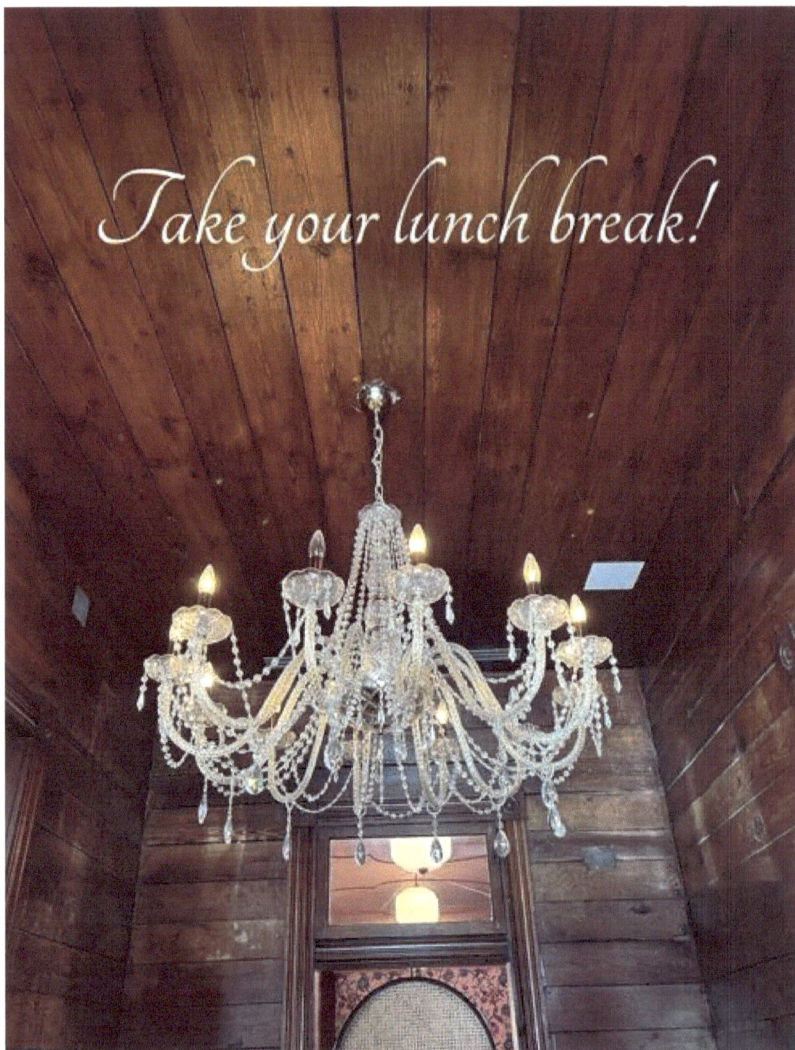

Take your lunch break!

# Take your lunch break!

Take your lunch break and be punctual. When you work a certain number of hours, it is required by law that you take a lunch break. Our bodies require food and water to function at our best. Plan for your lunch break, and meal preparation at home is not a bad idea.

Respect authority!

## Respect Authority!

Respect authority, respect your elders, respect yourself. You may not like what your boss has to say, but you do have to respect him/her. Never think that you can get away with being disrespectful at work, it will be addressed.

Integrity matters!

# Integrity Matters!

Integrity matters immensely. An employee must be honest and have good moral principles. A person must make the right choice, even when no one is looking.

Colossians 3:23

And whatsoever ye do, do it heartily
as to the Lord, and not unto men;
KJV

# 5 Year Goals:

_____

_____

_____

_____

_____

_____

_____

_____

_____

_____

_____

_____

# Plan Of Action:

_____

_____

_____

_____

_____

_____

_____

_____

_____

_____

_____

_____

# Areas Of Improvement:

_____

_____

_____

_____

_____

_____

_____

_____

_____

_____

_____

Jesus looked at them and said, "With man this is impossible, but not with God; all things are possible with God."

Mark 10:27

www.ingramcontent.com/pod-product-compliance
Lightning Source LLC
Chambersburg PA
CBHW041807040426
42448CB00005B/303